THE BROKEN UKULELE

Advice for Twenty Somethings
in a Broken World

Mark Hunter LaVigne

Rock's Mills Press
Oakville, Ontario
2020

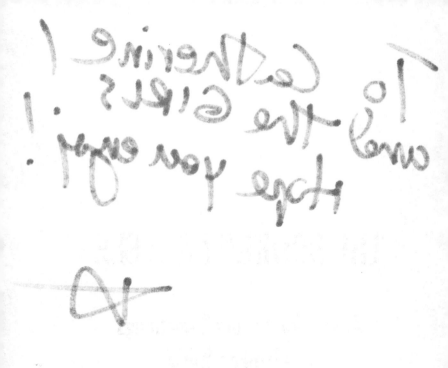

Published by

Rock's Mills Press

www.rocksmillspress.com

For information, please contact Rock's Mills Press at
customer.service@rocksmillspress.com

DAY 1

I had been preparing for years for my Algonquin Park solo, upping my backcountry skills on close to 30 trips, all by canoe and always with other people, primarily my sons and daughter, my best buddy, and his sons. Sometimes a friend, a few times a new Canadian neighbour to introduce him to Algonquin Park, my happy place of 7,500 square kilometres of provincial park about three hours north of Canada's largest city, Toronto.

But a solo is different, you are alone of course, camping in the wilderness by yourself. This tests you mentally, and despite all the years of preparation, I was rather scared that first night. And it is a lot easier going solo with a backpack than when you add a canoe to the mix. Even though my beaten-up used Kevlar is "portageable" by myself, I am no spring chicken to say the least, more like an fat old turkey! My very last backcountry bucket list will include a solo canoe trip somewhere in Algonquin, but maybe through one of the direct routes without a portage!

Another big motivation for the backpacking trip is to get my canoe kit down to a one-pack system. Our canoe trips include lots of fresh food, lots of wine, and other comforts such as chairs and tables. So getting to a one-pack system would mean an easier solo canoe trip in my future, as well as being able to team up with one of the boys and do canoe trips much deeper into the park, utilizing some very long one-, two-, and even three-kilometre portages. Carrying a canoe with a partner, one pack each, is feasible on these long portages, but not if we have to do two or more passes, as on our last canoe trip into Little Trout Lake with three portages totaling about 1½ kilometres. Times three, that was a lot of walking and hauling, although the amazing campsite, an island to ourselves, was worth it!

So I called the park, and asked for advice, and ended up speaking with a gregarious older guy who advised me about the best trips for someone of my age and shape, but also ones that would get me to a nice place. He admitted later in the conversation he is wheelchair-bound. So I was hoping for a really easy walk since invariably I once again had brought too much stuff, though at least all stuffed into one pack. What I ended up doing was only about six kilometres as the crow flies, but up the whole way (an elevation change of 500 feet/152 metres, with a total vertical of 1,000 feet/304 metres) and with an almost 70 pound/32 kilogram pack—that was far enough! This was all done in 85 per cent humidity with the temperature 80 degrees Fahrenheit/27 degrees Celsius.

So picture this middle-aged guy, excited as a schoolboy, going on his solo. Wearing his Tilley hat. Being 20 pounds overweight makes it all that much more of a workout. I got a late start since I stopped at a Mountain Equipment Co-op (MEC) on the way up to Algonquin, to purchase a much-needed water-purifying bottle, expensive, to augment my water supply. The map showed a stream halfway but I was not sure it would be clean. So that was my plan. I called my brother who lives near the store and whom I had not seen in ages. Typical North American nuclear family. He looks like a rock star, could have been one although never say never, and he joins me in this camping supply store with his long unruly hair scaring the clerks a bit. I find the water bottle I researched online and then spot it, the ukulele. Plastic. Meant to be indestructible, waterproof, etc. Popping into my head is the fact that although I play ukulele, and have two baritone ones (one for studio and one for campfires), they are at home. A baritone ukulele is played and tuned like a guitar, chord positions more or less the same, minus the two bottom strings. A smaller one, the ukulele in the store is concert-size, and requires different chord positions. Just the thing to help me spend my three days alone in the woods. I would finally have some time to learn the new chord positions. I had brought some song sheets with me (just in case) so had some music chords and lyrics anyway. So I bought the ukulele. Then I remembered I did not have a fleece in my pack, so bought one made by Patagonia, which when I set out I forgot in the truck along with a coil of rope I'd also bought there to hang the food pouch to keep it away from animals, including bears.

This brings me to two of my first pieces of advice, not that I am really qualified in any way to offer advice (I am a part-time professor, part-time musician, PR/media person in every bit of my DNA, but not a therapist or priest), but I'm offering it just the same because young people need lots of it. The world is broken in almost every way. So if you want to listen, I can teach you a few things that I've learned from my own mistakes, both about backcountry camping and about life.

May your home (or campsite) be filled with music of your own making.

It has taken me more than 40 years to learn to play guitar decently, then sing with it, write songs on it, and finally to actually perform live without pooing my pants. The many times my song-making has provided me with solace, with company, with a creative burst through my many moves cross-country, multiple professions, significant women in my life and at campsites have been priceless. I think once some people cheered after I was playing for a while at a back-country campfire (my kids will confirm this) but they were at the other end of the lake. It is never too late to learn an instrument and never easier than it is now to learn one with Google and YouTube. It provides an analog tactility to life, something that is missing these days.

I have become so passionate about the guitar that I built one, with lots of help—used a Martin guitar kit and had to replace the top, over-glued, and the neck, cracked. It took four years. I learned an immense amount about guitar construction, of course, but more from the 70-year-old-plus guys who let me hang out with them, Bill, Dave and Carl. During all of this I went through the WORST break-up of my life, the post-marriage one, which left me a slobbering broken-hearted teenager for almost two years.

Always try to build two benches with the same wood.

I have built benches. I love working with wood, as evidenced by my attempting a guitar build. I snagged some plans at Home Hardware, bought the relevant tools, and built my first bench (using hand tools) many years ago. Then I graduated to power tools, and built four more, augmenting the original plans. I spent lots of time sitting on them, usually late at night after the kids were in bed and my night shift at my computer was done, smoking tobacco (yes, I am an evil smoker and counsel you to quit, cold turkey, without vaping) and—you know—other stuff, and thinking about all kinds of things: work, songs, women, kids, wondering when the meteorite is going to wipe our planet off the face of the universe.... I call this "bench time." It is very precious time alone. This is where this little saying came from. *Try to find two purposes for doing something.* Building a bench provides you with somewhere to sit. A bench is also somewhere to think. And they can make great gifts, such as to aforementioned girlfriends.

So I get to the West Gate of Algonquin Park. I was so relieved when I booked my "interior permit" to see a site number assigned. This is something that always causes me "site anxiety" (SA for short) on canoe trips. A few times illegal campers have already been on a lake and we have had to push on and then be illegal ourselves. I am told this is happening more and more. People risk getting a huge fine. Not thinking about who they may be forcing to paddle another hour to find a spot to sleep! But site number or not, the two nice wardens tell me that no, there are no numbered sites on this little Maple Leaf Lake. So site anxiety comes rushing back.

My one and only official canoe-trip-guiding gig, as part of a large PR campaign, suffered from just such an illegal site occupation incident. We had to canoe another hour up a river to find a site and then set up in the dark and then cook dinner.

Back to my solo. I tell the wardens I did not bring my fishing rod, could not get my fishing licence renewed in time, and they laugh and say it is "free fishing" this weekend. Darn, another time-waster I could have used. Plus I only brought freeze-dried food and am not sure how that will work out either. The wardens give me careful directions and repeat them twice: turn left at the first left on the trail, follow it until you come to side trails, and then take a left, right, left, right, straight, right, left, and bingo! you will be there. Thankfully I *do* have a map.

I drive a short distance from the West Gate to a small parking lot off the lone two-lane highway that stretches from the West to the East Gate through beautiful, almost uninhabited wilderness. It takes about two hours to drive from gate to gate at highway speeds.

I park and then SA kicks in again—what if the lake is filled with illegal hikers? Day trippers? Young people who do not care? Older people who cannot go any further? I quickly pull out my pack, hat, and walking sticks. I put my pack on for the first time since I did the final load check and almost drop to the ground. This is a cliché in most backpacking books and movies and it is TRUE. You are so busy prepping, making sure you do not forget the most important things, that you over-pack. I even had a few more things to stick in the pack, but SA took over. So I forgot fleece, flashlight and my backup phone charger cube, the last two items both sitting in one little section of the truck's dashboard, awaiting insertion in the pack!

Off I go, beginning to wheeze pretty quickly. And thirsty very quickly. I walk only a short distance and take the first left. Check my map. Check the sign. And hiking we will go.

Follow the blue dots, Auntie Marcia, a joke that always made one of my buddy's kids laugh on canoe trips. It is Friday at two in the afternoon. The wardens said about two hours to get to my assigned part of the lake. So I allow three. There is a series of boardwalks. A vernal pond. My new hiking boots feel great, but I did work them out several times on a trail near my house. Then I realize I forgot my iPod. Okay, do not need that. Within minutes I feel the energy of the trees. I have experienced this all my life, being in a forest gives me energy. Walking in the woods, especially old woods, does something to my cells. Stimulates them somehow. The Japanese call this "forest bathing."

In not too long the sound of the highway disappears. But, of course, I am so driven by SA that I do not stop, do not enjoy the experience. In no time I am soaking wet. And the trail starts going uphill. I pass a side trail, but a quick check of the map tells me this is not the one I was told about, and it is to the right, not the left! One ravine is dried up. Of course, ravines by definition mean walking downhill and then uphill. The next ravine has a trickle. The next stream is very rusty looking, with a huge beaver dam blocking off a small lake. And you never, ever drink water near a beaver dam—

particularly downstream from it—unless you want a nasty dose of "beaver fever"!

Then I realize something. I have been walking for almost an hour. I have not seen another human being. When was the last time I did not see a person, hear a human-made noise for this amount of time? And then I realize how thirsty I am. I start looking for a higher spot where I can put my pack down so I not have to lift it up to get it back on—it is so freaking heavy. My water is inaccessible; I have the water bottles, which started out frozen at my house (ice is very heavy, Dumka), a leftover habit from my canoe-tripping days—you freeze everything freezable to keep the food in the food barrel cold. Then finally I hear rushing water. And come upon a fordable stream. And find a high place on a rock formation to put my pack down and easily get back into it. I do so successfully. Time for a break.

I guzzle a bottle of water. Completely ice-free now due to the heat. But so cold—so good. Then I light a cigarette, also so tasty. And then I think about my flask of bourbon and could use a little treat. So I open it up from the pack and have a very small sip—this has to be rationed carefully because I only brought one flask due to the weight and my lack of organization. Nectar of the southern American gods. I do like whisky. Here is some more advice for you.

Acquire a taste for bourbon (American whiskey) or rye (Canadian whiskey) or Irish whiskey or Scotch (officially only whisky made in Scotland and in a few places in Canada).

And of course, be very aware that whiskey is spelled differently, and that fact could actually lead you into a bar fight. The spelling *whiskey* is common in Ireland and the United States, while *whisky* is used in all other whisky-producing countries. Whisky made in Scotland is known as Scotch whisky, or simply as "Scotch" (especially in North America).

When I was a young journalist working in Calgary and living with my parents because the pay was ridiculously low, Henry, my dad's creative director (my father was a true *Mad*

Men-style advertising executive), showed up at the house. He was brilliant, and very Scottish. He said, "Laddie, if you're going to be a journalist, you have to learn how to drink whisky!" He brought a bottle of very expensive Scotch, I cannot remember which brand, and we sat at the kitchen table and by the time I was quite pickled, I liked Scotch. His advice was to buy the best you could afford and then drink it. With water on the side, no ice. He said a splash of water will "bring out the flavours." I have generally followed that advice for most of my adult life. Except this time. I take a nip of the bourbon my very talented writer mother-in-law recommended, without water. It is called Elijah Craig.

I then pull out my new purifying water bottle, get it working from the stream, and clip it to my knapsack. I then realize I forgot the rope I bought at MEC in the truck. Not again!

Time to keep moving as SA kicks in again. The trail starts going uphill quite steadily—up and down into gullies, and up again. The ukulele is in the bag that came with it strapped to the back of my pack, where the clerk at MEC said it would be safe.

After a long uphill stretch I find a rock to rest the pack on, put it down, and hear a "boing." Uh oh. I look in the little bag and see that the ukulele's machine head, where the tuning pegs are placed, is broken off. Shit! Crap! Poo on a bun!

I load my pack on my back and started walking uphill, then down, then up further, all the time thinking, MEC will probably take it back. But taking it back would be inherently dishonest. I broke it! Not a fair return. What a waste of time and weight. Maybe I could burn it in the fire?

But then I start to think, Okay, glass half-full. I do not have to learn new chord positions after all. And then start to think that *The Broken Ukulele* is a good title for a song, or maybe even a book. And then I start to think that a book about how to navigate through our broken world might make sense, might be needed. And then I begin thinking about my own broken world.

The profession I love, making news, both as a journalist and as a PR professional, is declining quickly as social media siphons off the advertising budgets that once supported the news business. The practice of "blogola," paying for positive reviews and posts, is yet another example of how the Internet's subculture of stealing and its general lack of morality are invading my beloved traditional media space.

Despite such negative thoughts, I cannot help but notice as I trudge along how beautiful this place is, how quiet, how fresh. I hike down into another vale and come to another stream and come across some fallen logs perfectly placed to take a break and slip out of my pack. So beautiful here.

When they built this massive park, the horse and buggy were on their way out and the automobile on its way in. I think about all of those employed as a result of the previous form of transportation—the horse veterinarians, the blacksmiths, the farriers, the stable hands, the buggy manufacturers, the streetcleaners—so many of them affected by the coming of the automobile.

Changes in technology like this are inevitable.

But I think how many industries have been broken by the Internet's subculture of not paying for things, or, more pointedly, *stealing* things, such as movies and music. How the advertising industry, which employed my father and me, has been entirely transformed. How me making news is now endangered. Yes, I had one of my best campaigns the summer before, but the past few years have been quiet as a practitioner, busier as a college teacher and as an author, but still an immense reduction in revenue to the point I had to sell my house.

I light a cigarette, partly to ward off the gathering mosquitoes, and realize that I have not seen another person for more than two hours now.

It is now about four in the afternoon and the heat is fierce, even under this forest canopy. I am soaked through, shirt and pants and hat. I finish my cigarette, shoulder the pack once again, and move uphill once again.

Several more uphills and little downhills, another stream crossing, this one slippery so I am glad to have the sticks for balance, and another uphill. Still have not seen another living soul—close to three hours now!

Up ahead, I see a clearing. Is it a lake? Am I finally here?

Nope. False alarm, it might have been part of a lake once but it is vernal now. And then another uphill. This one is the hardest. I stop several times, sweat dripping into my eyes despite my tight-fitting Tilley hat. I look at my water bottle; very little left and I am not sure how far my lake destination is away. My instincts tell me it is close. And one thing I have learned in my many years is to trust my instincts. And if they come as a *déjà vu* flash even more so. There was one time in graduate school I found myself bumped out of an apartment by my roommate's girlfriend. A high school friend knew of a vacant apartment in his enclave. Cheap. Close to school. So I arranged to meet him and check it out. The minute I walked through that door my warning bells went off. I went no further. And bailed. He was pissed off, probably was getting a deal from the common landlord if I took the place. A day later some classmates invited me to join them in their house a short walk from our offices and writing labs, so that proved to be a good decision!

Finally to the top of the hill. All hardwoods and then I can smell the water and feel it, catch a glimpse of a large lake. This must be it. Elation. My journey is almost over. Oh my aching shoulders and quads. Soaked through my clothes with sweat. Nothing better than a swim right now.

How good I feel at that moment. And then SA kicks in again and I start trudging. A sign announces the lake's name: Maple Leaf Lake. But no side trail yet. Head down, constantly looking for the tripping hazards of roots and rocks. The whole trail is like this. Fairly easy to miss the occasional blue dots on the trees directing you forward. Then suddenly, a side trail sign. I remember the warden telling me about that, so follow it to the left. A steep downhill, thank God for the sticks to help, and then into a deep ravine with some old-growth trees. They give off so much energy, these trees. A temperature drop of a few degrees. Then another side-trail sign. A boardwalk that the rangers must have put in with sweat and tears and then an uphill—not another one! And then a campsite marker on a tree and immediately after that an outhouse! In all my years of Algonquin backcountry I have never seen one of those in the backcountry. I peek in—

several rolls of toilet paper and then realize I forgot mine. So I naturally snag a few rolls and follow the path to the empty campsite. It is now about five in the afternoon. SA is driving me. The site is not bad, but on a marshy bay off the lake. Marsh means lots of mosquitoes in an hour's time. And noisy frogs. I do notice some firewood left, bless campers who do this, I have for years, always leaving a bit if possible for those who follow to make their first night a bit easier, or in case of extreme situations, even provide them with emergency warmth.

So I push on a bit and notice a huge tarp balled up by a tree. Then I see the campsite, vacant! It is up high from the water, relatively open on three sides. A nice breeze comes through even though it is not the windy time for Algonquin Park, which always seems to come at dusk. This is it! I ease off my pack not wanting to break anything else and do a jog. I made it! Look at my Marathon watch, the only Swiss-made Canadian watch on the market by the way, supplying military on both sides of the border for the past hundred years or so. THIS IS NOT PRODUCT PLACEMENT. The thing is indestructible. And accurate. And not expensive for a Swiss watch.

Celebrate life's little moments so you're ready for the big ones.

I go to my pack and pull out the flask of bourbon for a wee rationed sip. I sit on the log seat, light up a smoke, then light up another kind of "smoke," one which is finally legal in this country, and then at last pay close attention to where I am, in that moment.

The quiet is deafening. I have not heard anything human in more than four hours now, since moving out of earshot of Highway 60. I am surrounded by a mix of hardwood and fir trees, with enough of the latter to hear my favourite sound, wind through the branches. How I have consciously loved that sound since teaching campcraft skills at a choir camp when I was 18. Forty years ago, oh my God! how time flies.

First order of business now that my two smokes are done,

wanting another shot of bourbon but fighting the temptation because I am rationed, I take off my boots and socks. Oh what a feeling!

I then dig into the pack; my water shoes are somewhere inside. I toss everything out with abandon. Find the water shoes, take off my soaked pants, drape them over the rough-hewn log seat (thank you again, rangers) and stand up with some effort.

Okay, I want to swim. There's lots of time until dark—about four hours.

I look left and see a path down to the water, which quickly turns into a barely navigable cliff. So I descend, ever cognizant that if I fall and hurt myself, game over. If an older fat man falls in the forest on a solo backpacking trip in Algonquin Park, nobody may hear. I do not have a whistle around my neck! But at this point I do not care. I did remember to grab my Grayl water bottle to fill up. I get to the bottom with some effort, my quads are screaming. My shoulders are aching. And get to the shore rocks. I walk in and immediately sink to my ankles. Lots of detritus rises to the surface. Yuck. Stinky. So I trudge deeper. Now I am up to my knees in muck. So I push off and swim out a ways, leaving behind the muck. I fill up the water bottle. This device has limitations since I have to push the filter part into the bottle and need a hard surface to do that. I push a little bit in and hold the bottle aloft while I soak and drift a bit. I look up at the clear sky, a bit hazy, but the blue shows through and first I see a jet contrail and then hear the sound. Two thoughts go through my head almost simultaneously. "Blue, blue windows behind the stars, yellow moon on the rise, big birds flying across the sky" from Neil Young's "Helpless," a song I would have loved to play tonight on the broken ukulele. Secondly, outrage. How can jets be allowed to fly over this 7500-square-kilometre paradise? It should not be allowed!

Then I flash back to a flight coming back from Calgary when the pilot announced we were flying over Algonquin Park. I looked over my seat mate to see this massive green expanse and told her I had done many trips down there. She was medicated, I think, looked at me like a satiated deer with no comment. Then again, many people hate talking on airplanes!

I think then about swimming around the point, with my water-purifying bottle precariously held aloft, to see if there is a swimming area with a better landing. In retrospect I should have done so but for now think, Nope, let's get back up there. I make it to shore, get onto the rock, and then go through the laborious task of pushing down the water-purifying part of the bottle into the water captured inside the bottle—a lot of effort to get a cup of water. That done, I climb the cliff. A lot harder going up than going down. I will have to find a better water spot later!

Coming up to the site, I immediately get chilled. It is probably five degrees cooler than at water level as evening comes. Wet. Tired. I quickly find my shirt after realizing I had also left the fleece I had bought in the truck, along with the rope! Shit. The shirt would do, I guess, but I know how much the temperature drops in these Algonquin highlands at night, at around 1,800 feet above sea level—high enough to make a difference!

Once I get the tent set up and change out of my wet underwear, I will look for firewood.

I sip some cool clear water, and then get to work. I pull out the tent. A thought hits me hard.

Avoid debt at all costs.

I bought this tent, the knapsack, sleeping bag on sale last fall for 70 per cent off at MEC. I always buy on sale, or almost always, but am tricked by this consumerism. Now my debt is once again out of control. It constantly gnaws at me. And as I spend the last few months in my owned home, I must advise that a mortgage and a second mortgage are debt! And everything that goes along with home ownership, such as replacing crappy builder-grade windows and shingles and other issues. Vacations become just a memory. Plus often, to own these days, one must drive one or two hours into work—each way! If you lease, often you can get a better location, often a much better appointed place. At least enjoying our provincial and federal parks is very inexpensive, once you have the bought the gear.

I have broken another cardinal rule on this trip—always set up and test new camping stuff before you go! Well, too late now. But the tent goes up quickly and efficiently. The super-lightweight sleeping pad unfurls and self-inflates, with some help from me. The sleeping bag also, no issues, no tears.

Next, I use the little rope I do have to put up a clothesline. Off the wet underwear, into warm clean pants, and then outside again. The line sets up fast, and wet clothes are hung up to dry. And then to the firewood. It does not take too long to see that all the dead underwood has already been cleared out and burnt. So I go into the forest a bit deeper and find enough. Then I remember the wood at the other site. Phew, still vacant. Snag that. The previous campers at my site had left lots of kindling, thank you, so I can build a fire quickly. One of my favourite newspaper columnists is Roy MacGregor. He is a wonderful writer, and is especially good about writing about hockey, as well as canoe tripping. He is Canada's ranking expert on the legend of Tom Thomson's death on Canoe Lake, which is about 17 kilometres/10 miles of extremely rugged terrain and at least eight lakes northwest from where I am now. He once mentioned in a column the idea of leaving firewood for the next camper, and we have always taken that to heart. It actually could save a hypothermic camper, either canoeist or hiker!

Then onto figuring out the stove. It sets up pretty easily. I turn it on and fire the ignition and it fires up! Yeah. Now to find some water without climbing down and up that cliff. It is about six-thirty according to my Marathon so I better get moving faster.

I take a short break for another cigarette and think about tasks ahead. Get water for the stove. I used to be a better multitasker when I was younger or perhaps I never have been. At my age and experience, I do know women are wired to be better at this, at almost everything actually, especially public relations, but I carry on!

A man's version of multitasking is forgetting what he was doing and moving onto the next item on his Post-It note list.

I then remember my phone. I pull it out and turn it on and realize with horror it is at 15 per cent but that I do have one blip. Yes, for those under a certain age, that would have been the first thing done upon arrival, but for those of my age, other things took priority, such as cooling off and getting more water!

Anyway, I must have forgotten to charge it on the drive up. I only took a few shots on the way in. It is a refurbished old iPhone 5 because our twenty somethings keep wrecking their iPhones so I always end up either giving them mine or losing yet another upgrade. I notice two texts. One from my amazing eldest daughter Amalee and the other from my best friend Larry. Both wondering if I am alive. I take a few shots of the lake from the point. Sitting down, I remind myself to take it all in once again. So quiet. So beautiful. I do not hear another soul on the lake, not yet anyway. There are about nine camp sites on the whole thing, and since this is a back-packing lake, all sites are oriented to the trail as opposed to canoe trip lakes, which have their sites oriented to the water. This was a revelation to me!

I send two texts with a few pics and take some more shots. I put the phone into power-save mode and will look for the solar recharger later—the light is waning now so probably I can leave that until tomorrow. I then continue on my water mission.

In front of me is a cliff. I look down it, ten feet. Cannot go that way although there is a lovely flat rock ledge at water's edge which would be perfect for getting water and swimming. The water looks deep there.

I look to the right and see another path and take that to a sloping rock, which I carefully descend. I grab a cup full of water with my Grayl (minus its water-purifying part) and immediately slip and go down hard on my side, scraping myself in a few places. Ouch. Remember my earlier question: If a fat old man falls in the forest will anybody hear?

I refill the cup carefully and head up to the stove, pour it in, and repeat the process so my pot is now full. I turn it on, and the thing, as advertised, boils a litre in less than a minute!

I then ponder which freeze-dried meal to try and decide on the spaghetti with meat sauce. I carefully pour in about a cup of boiled water and reseal the bag, letting the water in the pot cool. This is much easier to do than push the darn Grayl down all the time! I still have my three empty water bottles from the trip in, so will fill those and let them cool overnight. Five minutes later I dig into my Mountain House freeze-dried meal. A little soggy, since I poured too much water in, but still so good, so hungry! I put that empty bag into the fire pit, along with the wax-cupcake Firestarter for later.

I decide to pour a wee bit of bourbon into my stainless steel coffee cup, add some precious water, and really savour it over another cigarette. Still so quiet. The wind picking up a bit, as it always seems to do in Algonquin around dusk. The mosquitoes are not too bad at all on this windy point camp-site, and the quiet still amazes me. I still have that Neil Young song in my head, definitely an earworm.

Enjoying my bourbon and water, I notice a little chip-munk touching my leg. "Hello, little buddy, where did you come from?" I actually say out loud. He goes up to the freeze-dried pouch and sniffs. Then he actually goes into my bourbon cup! I dig into my food pack, pull out one of the small bags of trail mix I got at Costco, and pour some on the ground. He quickly Hoovers up some nuts and takes off to his hole about ten feet away. Now I know where he lives!

I then take my food bag, containing only freeze-dried food, coffee and some Clif bars, and hang it from the clothes-line, fully aware it is not far enough off the ground or away from a tree to be secure if a bear or other creature visits, even though it is above a steeply sloping rock. But it should do.

By this point, the water in the JetBoil has cooled down enough for me to put it into the empty disposable plastic bot-tles I lugged in and consumed with abandon on the way. Hot to the touch, but not enough to melt them. I put them under the log seat where they will cool nicely overnight.

So important to either use a purifying device of some sort or boil your water to avoid picking up parasites. I had "bea-ver fever" when I was a counsellor in training on a canoe trip many years ago and I can attest it is not pleasant. Although Algonquin lakes are clean, naturally occurring parasites near beaver dams or other swampy areas can spread even into the centre of lakes and make you quite sick!

Dusk has now progressed into the gloaming, post-dusk/pre-night, a favourite time for me.

I get the Firestarter cupcake going and feed the fire. I notice how quickly the temperature is dropping and go into the tent to put a T-shirt on under my long-sleeve shirt and once again regret forgetting my fleece in the truck, although it would have added half a pound to the pack for sure! I also then look for my headlamp and cannot find it. I turn on the little tent light and in a panic look again. Nope, not there. Nor is a flashlight. How did I not transfer that from the canoe trip kit? With my phone almost dead, I may be out here without any light! But then my hand finds my hat with the small LEDs built into the rim. I reverse the small button batteries and the thing turns on full-strength. Thank God!

Better to have something when you don't need it than not have it when you do.

I should have brought my Canada Goose light down jacket, which would have been perfect! I quickly build the fire up, and savour its warmth.

I look up at the sky, waiting for the stars to come out. There was a wispy cloudiness earlier so we will see. I stand up and look back into the forest and that is when I notice them. Huge gaps in the trees that look just like two giant eyes, looking straight at me. It does not take much for my imagination to run wild. Are they indicative of an evil forest spirit? Is this why no one else is camping here, long known as a bad place to be?

I go back to the fire and think of all the fireside chats over the years with Larry, my kids, his kids, others.

I keep feeling those giant eyes on me. I look back. Yup, they are still there, the last of the light shining through them.

I look back at the fire burning down and realize how very tired I am. No stars out yet. The stars are always a wonder for me here, far enough from the city lights to truly shine.

I realize that I am quite bored with myself after only seven or eight hours! And those Forest Eyes are bugging me. So I decide to turn in early, only about nine-thirty. I spread the coals out, pee on the fire to put the last of it out, not wanting to waste any water, grab my Grayl water bottle, and quickly crawl into my tent and my sleeping bag and immediately warm up. Then I hear it.

Faint music at the north end of the lake. Canned, not self-made as mine would be had I not broken my ukulele. But actually welcome. I turn off my tent light and the dark comes instantly, with the sky still aglow with the last of the sunset. Sleep comes very quickly for this old man.

DAY 2

I sleep very well and sleep late, a luxury I generally cannot afford because of my business, which usually demands a 12-hour day, and my special-needs daughter, Maggie, who rarely sleeps past seven-thirty. Then it's a scramble to clean her up (if she had an accident overnight in her pull-up) get her dressed, fed, medicated and onto her transport to her day program.

When two weeks old, Maggie experienced a near-fatal series of seizures. We rushed her to a regional hospital, and then she was taken by ambulance to a children's hospital. We followed that ambulance and to this day, whenever I see one with lights blazing and siren blaring, I flash back to that moment. She was in intensive care for two weeks. On the first night, I could not sleep; I was in a rocking chair by her bedside and remembered a prayer taught to me years before by the Jesuits, "Maranatha," an Aramaic word that is only mentioned once in the New Testament, and roughly means "Come, Lord." We were taught it as a chant, to help meditate, and I started repeating it in my head in time with my breathing. I must have prayed like this for almost two weeks solid. On two occasions her condition grew so grave we did not leave her except to go downstairs to try to eat or to walk around the block. Finally one of the doctors told us that they had to take her off life support; they did not believe she would live, or, if she did, she would be a vegetable. Dr. Death, as we called him, walked away, and as we ourselves went down a spiral staircase several voices in my stomach told me she would be okay. I did not say anything to my wife at that time, fearing I had gone nuts. Later, talking with a trusted Jesuit I had known for many years, he said that is how the angels often talk to us, or, in Indigenous cultures, one's ancestors. We finally came to the last night before they were going to pull her off life support. I spent most of the night rocking by her bed, repeating "Maranatha" over and over, looking at her beautiful little face that was illuminated by a very bright light above her, trying to ignore all of the tubes running from her. Finally, a kind nurse gently convinced me to lie down in the nearby lounge where my wife Kim was sleeping. The next morning we slept late and a nurse came in to wake us. We had agreed earlier that we could not bear being there to see her intubated and die. We both jumped up and ran down the hall to where she was, her eyes open and responding to our voices. A very emotional moment to say the least. As we were walking down the hall, I went into the room where she had been during the night to say thanks and sit for a moment in that rocking chair. It was then I noticed that there was no light above her bed. And it *was* her bed, her chart still at the end of it. My faith has been deep ever since, and I continue to pray "Maranatha" as much as I can. Sometimes quite unconsciously. There is power in prayer, I can guarantee that.

A bit of an unreal feeling at first when I wake up—this is not my bed, this is not my room—oh yeah, I am by myself in Algonquin Park. And I am ALIVE! I sit up and see my phone on top of my pack. Before nightfall I did plug it into the solar recharger, which I had charged at home before packing it. Nothing. Dead as a door nail. So no camera, because I forgot to put my little waterproof Nikon into my pack!

We will worry about this later. First order of business is to go to the "thunder box," which I had found soon after setting up camp yesterday. A thunder box is a box with toilet-seat-sized hole cut out of it, where one does one's number two, and number one if you are so predisposed. I generally pee around my campsite in places to deter animals from visiting. It has worked for years!

I find the thunder box without too much trouble and find a toilet seat attached. Not only a seat, but a lid with a message written on it: *Please enjoy. Ed.* I do my business and have to laugh. On many canoe trips, given the marginal added weight of a toilet seat, I have brought one along with me and at the end of the trip have usually donated it to the site's thunder box along with a roll of toilet paper in a Ziploc. I wonder how many people appreciate the gesture? But I had never thought of fastening the seat down, bringing the screws to do so, leaving a message, or, for that matter, bringing a toilet seat along on a backpacking trip where I've tried to reduce the

weight of my pack as much possible, to the extent that I even forgot some essentials!

I still have not heard another human, apart from those playing music last night at the north end of the lake. I am in my underwear and a T-shirt and old camping Crocs and really have no motivation to change, although a swim would be lovely.

So my day's itinerary—as my late aunt's bodyguard at her posting in Jakarta used to say, "What is the program for today?"

1. Eat.
2. Find more firewood.
3. Find a better place to get water and swim.

4. Recharge phone with solar charger.

Not necessarily in that order. Eating is a priority. As I am firing up the JetBoil and prepping the freeze-dried breakfast pouch—yummmm, eggs and bacon—as well as coffee (a Starbucks Via pouch), I think of my late aunt and that trip she and the Canadian government gifted me after I had finished my undergrad, visiting her at her diplomatic posting in Indonesia. And how the times I was alone on that trip, in Bali and Bangkok, helped me grow up a bit.

Lina was a complete surprise. Although about my age, she was many years more mature, being a diplomat with the Brazilian government. Half Portuguese, half Japanese, so exotic, and so easy to hang out with. Although we were only together for four days, it seemed a lot longer. Our lovemaking was spontaneous, unhindered by guilt or any expectations. I had had many girlfriends by the time I met her, but this one I could tell was very special. I was only 23 at the time, and probably in many ways a young 23. But at that point, I took that lovely turn of fate for granted, not realizing that the universe does not send that many one's way, where it really clicks mentally and physically, where being with someone as is easy as being with oneself. Love takes practice, however, and after the eventual heartbreak, it takes a lot of work to open your heart again. And having it open is an essential signal to the universe that you are ready for love once again. At this stage in my life, I feel perhaps the universe gave me my last chance with Vera, with whom I fell deeply in love after my marriage ended. I deliberately stop myself from going down this path, of recognizing and regretting the opportunities I did have in life with special partners, including my ex-wife, whom I could not seem to make happy in our last years of marriage. Although is that one's responsibility, to make someone else happy? I do not think so. It is your responsibility to make yourself happy, and that starts with liking yourself, enjoying being alone with yourself, maybe becoming your own best friend! And doing this, my solo, is about enjoying myself, being by myself, allowing this ongoing conversation with myself to happen (not out loud, though, in case somebody does come along).

Being alone is not easy. Being alone without any technology is even harder. The fact that most of my technology is dead is fateful. I even took out my emergency radio to reduce weight.

There is so much noise in our world, not just physical, but also caused by too many channels of information rushing at us. One of the biggest offenders is texting. It is instant. Very useful. But also very problematic. How many times have I seen things explode at work or personally because of text's brevity, or email causing the same problems? Misunderstandings? Generational differences in meaning, for example "lol," can get you in lots of trouble! Often, simply picking up the phone or even better, walking down ten office cubicles, can solve an awful lot or avoid one heck of a shit storm!

There is no "con" in text.

This time I know not to pour too much water into the freeze-dried pouch; I then put two sticks of the Via coffee into my cup and fill it with boiled water up to the brim. Damn, really miss at least some Coffeemate. Product idea: sell powdered Coffeemate in the same format as these Starbucks sticks of coffee. Oh coffee! I close the seal of my freeze-dried pouch and shake it up and wait the requisite five minutes.

I open the pouch and gobble down breakfast. Not bad at all. I take one of the water bottles, pour it into the JetBoil, and get it going again to make some more coffee, busying myself with that for a bit. The next coffee goes down as well as the first and after a second visit to the thunder box I get back to the site and sit on the big rock to ponder my next move.

Well, that would be firewood. I always harvest dead wood, but I noticed yesterday that this area is quite cleared out, so in underwear, T-shirt and Crocs, I go deeper into the woods. Not a good idea! Always wear boots, long pants and a long shirt when doing this. But I am in a particularly wild man kind of mindset, I guess. Deeper and deeper I go and finally find a wind-shear scar where several big trees are down. I start harvesting with my fold-up saw, much better than a hatchet or axe and much lighter. After a while I have a large armful cut and make my way back, leaving the saw. Two more trips like this and I have a good fire's worth. I then go along the shore. On a canoe trip, you find some of the best firewood on the shoreline where trees have died and the parts above water are left to dry in the sun, often becoming bone dry in just a season. But you need a canoe for that, and two people ideally. Then I spy a dead fir tree, bone dry. But it's under a cliff in dense brush. I try to get to it, my saw in one hand, the other holding onto branches and rocks and things, which immediately triggers an earworm of the America tune, "A Horse with No Name."

Who needs earbuds when you have earworms.

I harvest a little bit of the dead tree for fire starter although I do have one Firestarter cupcake left. I get back to the campsite, dump that little tree top, sweating like an old bull. I notice lots of little forest nicks in my arms and legs, but thankfully I had packed work gloves and wore them, since a nick on a finger can inhibit guitar playing for at least a week!

I go look at the solar recharger and check the phone. Nothing. No charge. I plug it back in, change the setting, and hope it will get the thing going so I can at least get a sunset shot. I love sunset shots. I have them from all over Canada, my wee collection. "Kinda like those sunsets, that leave you feeling stoned," yup, another earworm. Blue Rodeo, "Hasn't Hit Me Yet." For me, the only way to get rid of them is to play the song on my guitar, or have one earworm knock out the other earworm. But yup, I broke my instrument.

It is now about noon and I am still in my T-shirt and jockey underwear and Crocs. Nice moment to maybe roll a wee joint! Although my bandmate Eric's advice to his kids pops into my head—"Do not make it your recreation" (an even more important message nowadays with it being legal in this country)—I still do so, go to my tent, grab the small Ziploc and go and sit on my campsite's big rock.

I have the Ziploc on my lap, trying to roll a small spliff

inside it so I do not spill any precious contents, when I hear an accented female voice ask, "May I come in and sit on your rock?"

I look up and there is a beautiful blonde young woman backpacker, her shirt pulled quite low by her backpack's straps and showing ample bosom, and I choke back a combination laugh and gasp of incredulity.

"Ah sure" comes out of my mouth, the first thing I have said out loud since I met the chipmunk.

I seal the Ziploc and stand up and realize I am not really dressed. She puts her pack down with a sigh and we introduce ourselves. She tells me her name is Amelie, and that she is from Germany. I am so excited to meet another human, and a gorgeous one at that, and go to my tent, put away the baggie, and pull out the one book I brought with me, Kristen Harmel's *The Room on Rue Amelie*, really too thick a trade paperback to take on a backpacking trip. I show her the book and ask what are the odds, and then also go into a babble about my eldest daughter being named "Amalee" and how we named her after a ski instructor I worked with years ago called Amalea.

I offer her water from my stash of boiled water in plastic bottles, now cool from the low temperatures overnight in these highlands, which she gratefully accepts and guzzles.

I find out she actually works at the park's visitor centre; there are lots of German tourists here. I tell her of the older guy we met some years ago on Joe Lake whilst on a canoe trip who could barely canoe, was wearing a long shirt with a hat, and had with him a fishing rod and a garbage bag, which we assumed held his sleeping bag and tent. Every year we see a middle-aged European male doing a canoe solo in this manner, a bucket list item for many it seems.

She laughed and noticed my meal. I can tell she is very hungry, so offer her a choice of meals; she eventually chooses one and after a short boil and simmer, gobbles it down, admitting that all she had been surviving on for her six-day solo was porridge and nuts.

Always be kind when you can, the universe needs it like oxygen.

This is being kind. A very simple thing to do. I have enough food to last me a few more days, just in case I get lost, and she is hungry. It is the kind thing to do. I have practiced this for years, it is simple, it makes me feel good, and is so easy. When someone in your path, or campsite, needs help, just be kind. Holding a door open for someone, giving up a seat to someone weary, letting someone cut in front of you in heavy traffic, it is all so easy. And do not expect a return on your kindness, although it often comes back at you threefold from the universe.

She is such an attractive young woman, blonde, almost Teflon blonde, blue eyes with glasses, incredibly clear skin and a charming, endearingly geekish way about her. I tell her I want to go swimming (obviously covered in sweat and dirty and quite smelly, I must add) but was afraid to go alone, and besides, could not find a decent swimming area. She stands up, and within minutes finds a concealed path that leads down the cliff onto a flat rock that is perfect. She excuses herself and goes into the woods and changes into a very small bikini and comes out. I decide to swim in my underwear although I do change into my water shoes. In we go. The lake is flat calm and we cannot see or hear anyone. And since it is a shallow lake, it is very warm, unusual for Algonquin Park where the lakes tend to be quite cold even in high summer.

On the way to the swimming area I get her to check out the solar-powered recharger; since she is studying science at uni and seems geeky I think she might have a fix. She ponders the connections for a while and says the device might be broken.

We swim out a ways and enjoy the beauty. Eventually we swim back and lounge on the rock for a while, drying off. We go back to the campsite and she goes into the woods to change whilst I just sit there in my wet underwear drying off. They are boxers so almost like a bathing suit. When she returns, she asks the time, I find my watch in the tent and she realizes she has only two hours until her pick-up time in the parking lot. With an exchange of email addresses, off she goes, leaving me at the campfire not really believing this actually happened.

I sit there bewildered. I realize that although she admitted she was in her late twenties, it is still way too young for a man of my age. I am even more acutely aware of my age now since I teach the same age group, a "no-go" zone for me personally, morally and professionally. But I realize how much I have missed human contact these past 24 hours. Like oxygen!

Where did the years go? I think about what I was up to at that brave young woman's age. A young reporter, eager and so energetic. Poor as a church mouse, so determined to succeed that I paid no attention to living in the present. Yes, I worked very hard, tried very hard. My first radio station was a clone of *WKRP in Cincinnati*, including a gorgeous receptionist who made more money than most of the rest of us. In the course of five years, I was in a new city every year, had blow-up furniture (bed, couch) that fit into one trunk. A guitar. A few books. I refer to these times as my "radio daze." I remember the missed romantic opportunities, the missed job opportunities and how one directional change may have altered my life, for better or worse. Flash forward 30-plus years and here I am, a part-time professor yearning for a full-time slot somewhere, anywhere, with a business struggling in the wake of the massive shift of budgets to digital advertising, leaving me, traditional news media and our democracy all gasping for oxygen.

The reason I did start up my own business was to be a better caregiver to my very young daughters, one struggling with severe special needs. I remember how awful and lonely I felt at my desk on those first Monday mornings of self-employment. It took me a while to also realize, as clients came to my company, how amazingly free I felt, apart from the fear of the business going down, a fear that has never left me. Entrepreneurship is wonderful, but it is also scary. I came up with this slogan shortly after going it on my own, printed it out and framed it.

The freedom far outweighs the fear.

Freedom also comes when you are debt-free. No more credit-card minimum balances to pay. No more student loans to pay back. No more car payments. And there is another freedom, from *stuff*. Keeping your life decluttered. Not owning too many clothes, or too much junk. Buying quality once, so it lasts forever. And believe me, I am so far from freedom from clutter it is scary, although I am trying hard now. There is a lots of advice on The Google about how to declutter, get rid of things, sell stuff.

Trying to bring all the essentials in a backpack is a great lesson in decluttering. But do not go too far (as I did on this trip) and forget some key stuff. Such as one of those blocks that recharge phones, or a good headlamp, although my LED hat light has done the trick so far.

One of the things I hear constantly from my own kids and students is the unaffordability of houses in our major cities. A mortgage is debt. We are led to believe this is a good debt, that we can sell in the end and use that money to retire. At this point in my life, after co-owning or owning three houses, it is much better to rent, closer to the cultural centre of a place, avoiding huge commutes, and the expense of a car or *two* (the reality of suburbia or exurbia), living in smaller spaces, with less stuff, and pouring that money into pensions and investments. One city in Canada that does it right is Montreal. It has a much higher ratio of renters to owners, always has, hence more rental housing much closer to the core, and that surplus money saved also goes into living— fashion, entertainment, eating out more often … this is the European way of living and after you travel there, hopefully at least a few times, you may see its allure. How many Canadians and Americans are house poor, meaning yes, they are paying down million- or multimillion-dollar homes far away from a city centre and have very little left over every month, or worse, go further and further into debt, borrowing against the house, to keep up a lifestyle that may not be viable any longer. We need a big shift in our North American thinking.

Whether a complete housing crash will cause this I have no idea. There are a billion people on this planet who can afford to live here, are buying up property at an alarming rate, and that is also not the answer. In coming years, we are going to see 100 million people on the move, escaping environmental or geopolitical disasters. We not only have to accommodate ourselves, but also them eventually. I must admit I am fascinated with shipping container homes, want one or two. Finding a place for them is the challenge! Learning the skills to augment them too—welding, electrical, plumbing skills. I can drywall well, after two teenage boys with a penchant for damaging walls!

I suddenly feel very lonely so I strip out of my wet underwear and find a fresh pair. Put on some pants and shirt and decide to go and find some more firewood, trudging further afield, maybe even meeting some more people?

This time I hang a left onto the trail outside my campsite and go for a wander with saw in hand. After a short while I come to more of the boardwalks incredibly built by the rangers over swampy areas. These ones go on for a long way. Passing by pristine wetlands, the water so clear and pure. At one point I have a beautiful view of the lake, like a postcard, so hard to take a bad picture here. I come back to this very spot almost exactly a year later to get the picture on the opposite page, since my phone is dead.

I keep trudging, my eye scanning for deadwood tucked away, missed by the plethora of other hikers, always looking for a dead birch, my favourite campfire wood, skinny and soft enough to process easily, hard enough to leave lasting coals.

I keep hiking, leaving the boardwalk and heading back into dense, thick, old second-growth woods. Hard to imagine a lot of this vast 7,500-square-kilometre park was at one point logged of its old growth to feed the building boom in Canada as well as in the US, England and Europe. These woods are so dense, it is hard to hear others from the trail side; I suspect I have already passed the campsite with the music I heard last night. That seems a long time ago. Still there is no one on the trail. One of my quirky fantasies while backcountry is that we come out from a few days of being

completely unplugged and find no one, just abandoned cars and buildings. Everyone gone. Vanished in some apocalypse. I am sure this theme has been done before. Just the same.... I took my emergency windup radio that also has a built-in USB charger out of my pack after my last weight check at home. I make a mental note to at least fit a small transistor radio into my pack on the next trip. For storm warnings if nothing else.

I am walking fast, my stiff quads loosening up from yesterday's hike, was that only yesterday? Someone asked me once why I like going into Algonquin's backcountry. One of the key reasons for me is that it slows down time. A day seems like two or three in the city. A two-hour drive in the big city flies by, but a two-hour hike here seems two or three times as long. A weekend seems like a week.

Whereas time in the city, in my up-to-recently very busy career, would fly. So fast, here I am almost 60, when many I know are retiring from their education or government jobs, with full pensions, and I have nothing. Caregiving for my special daughter and others is a big reason. The fact I needed to be home for Maggie, which did limit my income potential, and always believing my ex-wife's pension would get us through in later years. Well, that went poof. And left me at my age with no pension, with my core earning potential gone thanks to Facebook and Google now sucking up 70 per cent of marketing communications budgets.

What this has also done is created a conduit for fake news, manipulated news, disguised news. What is not taught in school much, and it should be core curriculum from grade one onwards, is what is real news, how is it gathered, how is it made, by whom, and where can you get it. One of the key things a major newspaper (or local one for that matter) does is to tell you what you *should* know, not necessarily what you *want* to know. When you have multiple filters on your news feeds, you are barely getting a news feed at all! And knowing what sources to trust, such as news agencies like The Canadian Press—that is *real*. So are *The Globe and Mail*, *National Post*, *Toronto Star*, the *Toronto Sun*, we are blessed in our metropolis to have four dailies! Other news agencies that are worthwhile news sources are The Associated Press, Agence France-Presse, and Reuters, which sadly has been slowly diminished over many years. And understanding news bias, including what country it is from. Real journalists pay their dues, often taking at least a decade on the job to get into senior positions. The training in school and afterwards is intense, on the job, and often dangerous.

With traditional news, which was built on a model of selling advertising to fund its core product, seeing massive, never-ending budget cuts, this essential watchdog of our democracy is in severe jeopardy. When it's gone, it's gone. With this degradation come the leaders we see popping up all over the world.

I have made my living from one side of the news fence or the other my whole career. I am not a victim, I saw this coming, but cannot participate in fake news, or blogola, where the fence between earned information and paid information is completely blurred and broken down.

But what amazes me in this age of news disruption is that we swallow hook, line and sinker the metrics fed to us by Google and Facebook. In the previous model, there were independent third party groups that audited data, so one could get *true* data, not self-promoting data, however slick looking, provided by the specific media channel justifying the spend!

Truth is very subjective and complicated. If you want *true* news, read as much as you can from credible sources, newspapers and their online entities, trusted online sources such as the CBC and the BBC. A free marketplace of ideas, a concept several hundred years old, will help *you* determine what is true.

The truth is like a 1962 multi-sided nickel. It has many edges. But only two sides—heads or tails, fake or real.

I trudge along and feel like that buggymaker must have felt like, back around 1898 when the automobile was coming. That smart buggymaker knew a big change was coming. But he relished his craft. Was very good at it. Made a good living from it. But within the space of 20 years, his craft was gone. The same for all those who worked with horses. Gone. The emerging automotive industry gave rise to new factories, millions of jobs, and provided the impetus for other industries, such as oil for automobiles! Massive disruption.

Now we are seeing disruption that makes that shift look like junior kindergarten.

Any person in the middle could be eradicated and replaced by AI software. There will always be a need for the personal touch, at least for now, but many professions—lawyers, accountants, real estate agents, car salespersons, anyone in the middle—are in jeopardy. Retail is heading for huge disruption, in fact is already in the middle of it. Autonomous vehicles will change the car industry. Robotics, the next big wave enabled by AI, will change many more industries.

Two ways to prepare. Stay in school as long as possible

without accruing crushing debt and choose professions that will be needed by an aging demographic, a huge wave of migrants, and to help those replaced by The Machine. Education is a good choice. Extended health care another.

And once again, choose a profession—in the public sector if you can—that has a good pension plan. You may have to retire early, but at least you will be able to retire.

This all leads to another witticism, maybe.

Money can buy time, but time does not necessarily buy money!

What the hell do I mean by this one? Well, time can "make" money. If I had stuck to what I had started (a friend got me going but then changed investment companies and the automatic withdrawals stopped), I would have a million or more invested by my age. Enough to yield a retirement income. The Wealthy Barber, who was first interviewed on radio by me, back in the days when we still used tape, offers a few very simple and very wise pieces of advice: Put 10 per cent of every pay cheque into investments of some kind. And when you buy a house (if you buy a house—I am not convinced this is the way to go anymore), rent out part of it to cover your mortgage.

I further this by encouraging any young professional to go into public service, at whatever level, federal, provincial or municipal, in whatever form. Pay the maximum into the pensions offered. By my age, you can happily retire.

It took me years to realize how much I like teaching, although I have done it from a young age, as a poorly paid ski instructor, teaching campcraft skills at camp, and then, after a long hiatus, guest lecturing on public relations and then actually teaching my discipline of media relations and publishing three books on it. Teaching is honourable, and at whatever level, but if full time, the job comes with an excellent pension. But more than that, teaching gives of yourself, as well as allow you to learn things from your students. And if you do it right, you can have summers off to do things like this right now, walking in the woods by yourself, looking for firewood. With a song in your head constantly.

The sun is getting closer to the horizon and it is time to head back to the campsite and have a drinkie-poo, a pre-dinner cocktail of bourbon and some water, and I can then decide on which freeze-dried meal to have for dinner: rice and chicken; beef stew; lasagna with meat sauce....

Still not a soul on the trail or any noise, I wonder if the campers at the north end are napping. Another thing I strongly recommend you develop is the ability to nap. Many greats in history have done so, including Winston Churchill, JFK, and Thomas Edison. It has taken me years to refine this skill, to lie down for 15 to 20 minutes, usually after lunch or mid-afternoon, not necessarily every day, go right out and wake oneself up. Sometimes if I am fighting a bug I will nap longer, but that usually does the trick. Ironically, I have not napped on this trip, but have gone to bed super early.

Another song pops into my head, Stealers Wheel's "Stuck in the Middle with You." "Clowns to the left of me, jokers to the right." So speaking of politics, this is where we are as a country, Canada, right now, while looking east. Where the hell have all of these bozos come from? What the hell happened?

I hear many times from young people how disconnected they are, at least since Obama. I agree with them. But I also remind them that Gen Y and Z combined, in North America, makes up almost 40 per cent of the voting public. In other countries in the world, much more, although there are so few real democracies left. Then I hear that there is no one useful to vote for! And then I say to my kids or students, "Well, get engaged, join a party, or make a new one"—most people I know are socially left and fiscally right, with a bit of green in them, so what party nails that one?—"and get going. GO FOR IT. VOTE. RUN for office. FORM a new party if you have to or bring one of the established parties left or right or sideways, whatever suits you. YOU are the brightest, most educated, and frankly, most beautiful generation (or two) in the history of our species. The world is your oyster if you want to crack it open. PLEASSSSSSSSE."

I find myself hyperventilating a little on the trail. I really do need a drink. I meander back to my campsite.

I have several things to do at once and kind of freeze a little. Men, at least men of my vintage and experience (perhaps I really did party too much in the late '70s and early '80s, and the '90's too), often have trouble doing several things at once, where women of my age constantly amaze me at what they can get done in five minutes!

The modern reality of multitasking is that our response to workflow exceeds our ability to process the information.

But I persevere. I pull out and fill up the JetBoil. Get the food bag off the clothesline. Take off my hiking boots and socks and slip back into my Crocs. Sit down on the log (next time I am investing in one of those lightweight backpacking chairs) and pour myself a very small amount of bourbon, since I am down to the last of the flask (DARN). I visit with Chippie, so named since my kids called a chipmunk that hung with us for years at our rental cottage in the Algonquin Highlands the same name. I did not tell them that each year it was a new Chippie, like Chippie 1, Chippie 15, Chippie 20.

But chipmunks are amazing little animals, and one saved my life once. When I was about 13, I was allowed to hang out with some older boys in our neighbourhood. The pastime was to dig huge forts in the ravine at the bottom of our street. These boys were industrious, and had dug a large cavern into the side of a steep hill from the inside wall of the fort. They left earth pillars inside the cavern to hold up the weight of the roof. Even at that age I had my qualms about the efficacy of this plan. My job was to sit in the fort outside the cavern (a large hole covered with logs and grass with a side entrance), take the buckets of earth handed to me from the cavern entrance and then dump them down the side of the hill outside the main door. I was grabbing a bucket when a chipmunk (there were many in the forest around us) came into the fort, ran up one of my legs and down the other and then outside the door. Of course I followed and that chipmunk ran towards me, then away, drawing me away from the fort entrance. I was perhaps 100 yards away when I heard a large rumble and a cloud of dust came out the door. I rushed into the fort and there were my friends, all three, at the cavern entrance with their legs covered in earth. They had come looking for me as the buckets backed up. That chipmunk had saved our lives, or at least the boys in the cavern!

I feed Chippie a few nuts and get the JetBoil going. Select the meal du jour, pour in the right amount of water, seal and shake, and enjoy my very, *very* small bourbon and water. Each sip savoured. And listen to the wind through the pines trees, oh how I love that sound, one of my favourite sounds since I became conscious of it whilst teaching campcraft at a choir camp when 18, although at that time, my singing voice then was in baritone mode, it took years to get to alto. I would sit on a pine-tree-covered hill and hear that wind sound all day long. The choir campers would come to me to learn fire prep and building, simple cooking (hot dogs on a stick, then dipped in peanut butter). That was also the place I saw my one and only UFO.

On the last night of choir camp, I did my usual ghost-story circuit, telling the kids scary stories (which often helped them to sleep, ha ha), and was walking from the sleeping lodge to the dining hall when I noticed a bright light just above the hall's porch roof. I asked myself "When did Daryl [the camp maintenance guy] install that"? I had not noticed that light before. I stared for a while, and then the light zipped off at an incredible speed. I shrugged and entered the hall where our end of camp party was well underway. They all stopped and my camp director asked where I had been. I said just outside, and Phil said he had gone to the sleeping lodge and could not find me. Weird, I thought. Later I read about people losing time in UFO encounters. I did not have a watch on to corroborate that possibility. I also found out later that the choir camp is in the bottom corner of a supposed UFO triangle. Hmmmm. Play theme from *The Twilight Zone* (the original one).

Now, as the sun is closer to the horizon, one hand-width, the wind picks up. The sun is warm, the sky is a brilliant pale blue. The last of my current cupful of bourbon and water drains. After a while, I remember I have dinner simmering, open the pouch and gobble that down.

Despite yesterday's heat and humidity, it cooled down fast last night. Not tonight, it seems, but it is cooler, so I go and put on my long-sleeved shirt.

Time for another drink. And spliff. And to prep the fire. I build it around my last Firestarter cupcake, an amazing invention for dry or wet weather. Still a little early to start the fire, but it's built now. I sit back on the log, take a sip of my bourbon and water, I think there is enough in my flask for one more. Do I ever miss my glass or two or three of red wine by this time of day. Then it hits me. I can put a three- or four-litre bag of wine in my water hydration pack and carry that in front next time! When I get home, I will have to find that pack. Perfect.

I boil another litre of water on the JetBoil; now that I know a good water source without sliding off rock faces, that is easy. I still have a cooled-down water bottle left for nighttime (when I am often thirsty) although I am well hydrated now. A minute later, or less, the water boils, and I let it cool down.

I sit there, pondering this aloneness thing. How after my marriage ended, although I had three teenagers in the house, how lonely I was. Lonely for a partner, whom I had lost because I could not keep her from walking out the door. Another earworm pops into my head, but as a fragment, I think from a Doors song.

Learning to be alone is very hard for many people and like everything else, it takes lots of practice. Part of being alone is forcing yourself to hang out with yourself. Maybe the next step is allowing yourself to like yourself. Warts and all. Without earphones stuck to your head or being buried in a book or on your smartphone. A blessing my phone died and the solar recharger broke. A wise nurse told me that "glass half-full" is a good philosophy, this from a career trauma nurse who had seen much sorrow. But she also added that "it is important to keep filling that glass."

I take an extremely small sip of my water and bourbon, and light up yet another cigarette. And pay attention, despite the earworm, to the gloaming. The sun is below the horizon now and no sunset is apparent yet. Glad the phone is dead so I do not miss a sunset shot! Little do I know.

My only regret from the day (after Amalie had left, that is) is that I did not go for another swim in the surprisingly warm water (for Algonquin). Water is so important, swimming a gentle and therapeutic exercise I do not do enough! Or take enough baths, so therapeutic, especially with Epsom salts, something I will make time for when I get home to soothe my still-aching shoulders and quads.

I finally start my small fire. And then the wind picks up fiercely, sending sparks toward my new tent! I make the fire smaller. I love campfires, but when alone they lose their appeal for me. The campfire, my eldest daughter Amalee says, is "her happy place." I think for the conversation. For the guitar playing. I still have in my canoe equipment barrel a stick one of the boys fashioned. Bent at the handle. Carved by many hands. I call it the "talking stick" and we used to pass it around the fire to talk. It did not go over too well really, but was a good idea rooted in Indigenous culture. It also serves as a good fire poker.

I pour the last of my bourbon, a thimbleful really, into my cup and add some water. Staring at the fire, burning brightly because of the Firestarter cupcake, small, protected from the wind by a rock bigger than it. This keeps me occupied for a bit. The song "Five Hundred Miles," the traditional one from the Depression days, pops into my head and then a reminder to keep writing my canoe song to the rough melody and chord structure of that traditional song that I used to sing in brighter days with all of the boys on our canoe trips. I have to finish that one. I drain my last drink and puff my last cigarette of the night. Time for bed, and the stars are just starting to peep out. I quickly disperse the fire and pour some water on it. I am too tired and perhaps too bored with myself to stay awake any longer.

I *DO NOT* look at the woods in case those giant eyes are there again. I crawl into the tent, take off my pants and get into my sleeping bag. The tent glows from the last of the light. I am asleep before I know it.

DAY 3

At three-thirty in the morning I am awakened by a baby bawling! I know the time because I still have my watch on with its luminescent dial. The bawling baby is very close to my tent. I sit up, turn on my tent light, and listen to the bawling sound recede in the distance quite quickly. Then I remember this is the sound rabbits make when they are being murdered. Obviously it is a fast four-footed killer, likely a wolf. The bawling goes on for a long time, until it is finally too far away. I lie down, leave the tent light on, and go back to a deep sleep, with my knife and hatchet within easy reach. Why don't they invent a tent made from Kevlar that is not easy to bite or scratch through with sharp teeth or claws?

I wake to bright light and am so hot! Check the time, nine-thirty! That gives me only 1½ hours to pack up before the 11 a.m. "suggested" departure time, something I am rather anal about.

I make myself a double coffee, eat the last of my Clif Bars, think about a swim but am worried I do not have enough time (silly me) and so break camp and pack the knapsack. I have to do it a second time to get everything in. And find out later that I did it all wrong!

The best way to pack a backpack:

- Sleeping bag at the bottom.
- Base clothing on top of that.
- Sleeping pad and liner on top of that.
- Food sack and tent, the heaviest items, go on top of that, side by side. On top of that your stove, rain jacket, other clothes.
- In the cap or lid, that floppy part, you can store smaller things like phone, flashlight, chargers, saw, etc.
- My pack has two side pockets, one reserved for a musical instrument (turns out my Martin backpacker fits in perfectly for my next trip) and on the other side I put my freeze-dried food sack and water bottle holder.

Next backpacking trip I will put the three litres of wine in a front hydration pack, which also holds bug spray, bear spray, and the marine horn.

Knapsacks are amazing things. Smaller ones help organize one's life! I have one for my teaching gigs, one for weekend travel, one for my harmonicas and percussion, one for my bicycle stuff and want to add another larger carry-on one too.

Marine horns are great. They scare away animals and also can be heard much better than a whistle. As a testament, two 16-year-old Scouts who got lost on another part of this trail and smartly stayed put, could not be heard very well with their whistle because the forest on this trail is so thick! A marine horn would penetrate much better. After three days, they were found by an OPP police dog, which thankfully did hear their whistle. I will also look for emergency satellite beacons on sale to add to my kit, especially if I am solo and need help!

Once everything is in the pack again, I visit Ed the thunder box one more time, leaving my pack leaning against the log. I do my business and walk back into my campsite where a man and a young girl are standing. He asks politely if I am leaving or coming and I respond that I am leaving. I look at my watch and see it is precisely 11 a.m. Ha ha, my "analness" of being ready pays off. I then point out a full load of firewood, which he appreciates. Yeah Roy MacGregor! The man tells his daughter they just snagged the best campsite on the lake, which I had stumbled upon by luck! The man leaves his daughter with me as he goes to get the packs left behind, likely at the trail junction. When he returns, I notice his trimmed-down pack. For the next hour we share Algonquin Park stories and he advises me on how to reduce pack weight. He turns out to be a military policeman, a tough job, and talks about how Algonquin re-centres him every time. I have to agree. He admires my solo attempt, something he wants to do some day.

We part with a warm farewell, as I show him where the rest of the dead pine tree is on the shore cliff.

I walk for about five minutes, still feeling a bit stiff in the quads, make a wrong turn almost immediately but correct, and off I go.

After a big uphill climb I then realize the rest of the trip will be mostly downhill back to the parking lot. I meet a young woman soloist at the major stream, roughly halfway home, where I take a break. She does not talk, and has the determined look on her face I must have had whilst hiking and in full-fledged SA mode.

At a certain age you realize it is downhill from here, which is not necessarily a bad thing.

What an easy trail now, am loving it! Despite a few uphill parts out of ravines, it's mostly downhill. I suspect this part of the Western Uplands Trail was designed as the outbound part, and that the beginning, where I would have continued straight if I were on a longer trip, is much easier (this fact is confirmed by a buddy later).

I then meet a young couple, he looks half-Jamaican and perhaps half-Russian, she is half-Asian and perhaps half-Italian (the amazing multicultural reality of Toronto is our offspring, beautiful, brilliant, bringing us the best of the world) and they tell me a tale of a bear, their eyes big as saucers, this being their first backcountry trip. "Right in front of us," he says, "there was a bear." She says, "He looked at us, we at him, and then he made a humph sound, and took off into the forest at a gallop." I ask when they had seen him, and realize that if I had not taken the time to palaver with the military policeman and his daughter, I would likely have walked smack into that bear. I forgot to mention, I forgot my bear spray!

Then a fast-approaching group of young men, carrying a cooler, come up behind me. I tell them about the bear. They curtly say they know already and pass me at a brisk pace, oh to be young again! I think these were the music players at the north end of the lake. I then think, ah, bear bait! I start to play with the tortoise and the hare fable and drop the idea.

Finally I can hear the highway, actually a welcome sound. And then I am on the boardwalk knowing I am close. Quickly I am at the bridge and then into the parking lot and then at my truck. Relief. I guzzle the last of my water after dropping the pack into the back seat. I plug in the darn phone. Start the truck and I am on my way. Past the West Gate and its giant Canadian flag. Lots of issues with recharging the phone because of Car Play fighting with Sync, but eventually I get the phone going and call my daughter who had texted me about 100 times after my phone died.

And then I realize I have done it again. I have forgotten the now and become immersed in tasks, multitasking, the plethora of minutiae that comprises our modern lives. No longer alone, but even when I am totally alone, I am obsessed with what's next. Slowly more buildings appear on this winding road. Still not much traffic on this ribbon of highway that cuts through vast tracts of wilderness. It is the same size as some European countries. But the traffic slowly increases, as does the number of buildings. Then a small city, then cottage country. A two-lane divided highway evolves, then more smaller cities and then some bigger ones. More phone calls. The seemingly abruptness of wilderness trail, with not a soul, then some people, then more, then a highway, then a cell signal.

Maybe the whole goal of this story is to point out my many flaws and mistakes so as to help you (I hope) not to repeat at least some of them. This is perhaps the goal of many parents, many teachers? I hope I have given you some hope, and even a framework for a better life.

I'll give you the shell, you fill in the yolk.

An easy 2½-hour drive home, into the arms of my welcoming twenty somethings (sic), and into a BATH. Seems like I have been away for a week, not just three days. I cannot wait for the next time I can go into The Park. I will pack better, and not forget so much. After my bath, then shower and shave, with a huge glass of red wine by my side, I take out the broken ukulele from the side pouch of my pack and hang it up in a guitar hanger on my home office wall. This will constantly remind me that my glass is half-full. And to get writing this wee tome.

I hope my advice has not been too pedantic. And that you get yourself on a solo backcountry trip when you have built up some skills. Please remember, dear reader, you have so much good going for you. You will fix our current micro- and macro-problems, as well as the new ones that will arise in the future. I have just realized my wine glass is less than half-full, so I best run upstairs and fill it up. Hope to see out there in the backcountry!

About the Author

Mark Hunter LaVigne actually took this selfie on his solo backpacking trip to Maple Leaf Lake in Algonquin Park.

He has taught three generations of college-aged people by now (Gen X, Gen Y, and now Gen Z) as well as helped raise four twenty somethings. A few still actually live with him.

He is the author or co-author of four books: *The Adventures of Matilda the Tooth Fairy*; *Fundamentals of Public Relations and Marketing Communications*; *In the News* (third edition); and *Proactive Media Relations: A Canadian Perspective*.

He is also a songwriter and performer on guitar, ukulele, harmonica and vocals. He wrote four of the eight songs on *Out of the Woods*, by The Coyotes, and has an EP ready for release with some more of his songs. He likes to put them under the Christmas tree for his loved ones.

He lives in Aurora, Ontario with aforementioned grown children, and his buddy cat Simba.